SLIPCOVER

Haim Mizrahi
&
Joanne de Simone

authorHOUSE®

AuthorHouse™
1663 Liberty Drive
Bloomington, IN 47403
www.authorhouse.com
Phone: 833-262-8899

Published by AuthorHouse 03/05/2021

ISBN: 978-1-6655-1908-3 (sc)
ISBN: 978-1-6655-1910-6 (e)

Library of Congress Control Number: 2021904547

Print information available on the last page.

Any people depicted in stock imagery provided by Getty Images are models, and such images are being used for illustrative purposes only. Certain stock imagery © Getty Images.

This book is printed on acid-free paper.

Because of the dynamic nature of the Internet, any web addresses or links contained in this book may have changed since publication and may no longer be valid. The views expressed in this work are solely those of the author and do not necessarily reflect the views of the publisher, and the publisher hereby disclaims any responsibility for them.

COVER ART

"Music Sheets"

48"x48" Acrylic on Canvass

by Haim Mizrahi

To my mentor, Alan Planz...
- Haim Mizrahi

For the Magician...
- Joanne de Simone

Poetry is the crown of the passage...

- H. M.

*I*ntroduction

*I*f the mind is a trap for memories and flashing recollections, or a place that snatches a thought or action from the air for just a moment, this compilation of poems from the respective minds of two artists, sitting in a studio at East Hampton's public access televison show, Haim Mizrahi's HELLO, HELLO, reveal that minds meld and the instinctive floating grey cells give way to the unexpected whether it's on Joanne's paper scraps or Haim's laptop screen.

In the end, they are notable to the extent that they reveal what's under the SLIPCOVER.

- Joanne de Simone

All the poems in this book were written, spontaneously, on the air, live in the course of one year

Temper

Roaches of thought full of option burning
Coarse hands lend
And allow the spirit of compassion
To love thy self
To drop yourself down
Into the draining capability
Of sight and sense
And a prolonged challenge of fiction
Well and stable
And a hero in silence takes aim
At The moving letter on its way to rapture
Shows a self recognition like forefathers
Climbing ever so creatively they are
Above a concept of bright and a clear transparency
Up-to-date is the moment of initiations and delight

- Haim Mizrahi

$\mathcal{S}$UNDAY LOST

Places, spaces,
Strangers' faces
Misplaced...
Empty Sunday,
Vacuum sealed
Choir voices,
Octave choices
Displaced...
Empty Sunday,
Mimosa brunches,
Pigeon, parks,
Twilight, midnight,
Feelings frost
Sunday lost.

- Joanne de Simone

$\mathcal{F}$ree Ideas of Knowledge

Ending a shaky resolve it's not at fault
Needs a curve to hold the margins if yes
Trust of words leaning in the frontal prey
The teeth are milky at This stage
The grip lacking a resolve and intimacy
Rail slave turn of time slots purposeful
Haphazardly meaning the tone ring
It's a symbol of the relentless the soul
The Arrival cross world packers of slurs
Scream for the purchase of time and lasting
Engulfing the wind charging and crawling to victory
The overboard belittlement the sing along of whisper
Gorging a free approachable hymn one brought the
Seeking of country of birth now a new appearance
Froze parallel brinks a story of high packed action
Greatly sliding in the matter of live to begin with
A speed reducing vehicle of deep emotions
No pleading for the brief enchantments
Lower than the clarity of wills unite
Pleasure of aid helping ideas of knowledge
Slowing down frequently knowing the reasons
Ahead of the curve of an abundance
Plenty of skin rubbing scent blending odor bending
Soul sharing spearheading cross sharing
Elements of the love story of stages of love
Curving crowding picking a side of finality
No in no out no out no out no in no in has been

- Haim Mizrahi

WALLS

The pale walls look fatigued
From the loneliness,
And from the anticipation as
I twirl my feathered quill,
Humming a tune off-key,
Relentlessly waiting for,
Longing for the inspiration,
The motivation to tell you...
That it was you that allowed
The walls to crack and peel...
By your design it created
My new friend, named Alone.
But, Alone is lonely too,
His only friend is Despair.
And for my joy, neither care!

- Joanne de Simone

The loop

Bark and tongue dropping accepts a remorse
And the image drops one level and slow embankment
Civil relations in charge of positions to serve
That which provides us an acknowledgment
A bit delayed and somewhat precautious
Oriented and directed to the loop of length versus safety
Standing still bleeding the glare one extra to shine independently

- Haim Mizrahi

THERE IS NO MUSIC IN HELL

There is no music in hell —
Lucifer weeps at its loss,
Longs in vain for the harmony.
Without love's percussion and strings
The silence is a pernicious pall,
Deadly dark in the lonely Demon's den.
Heaven's song will not descend
To the inferno of deserted love —
When love's prize is snatched
By a wayward shallow scoundrel,
Your new home is a soundless Hades
Stilled to the meter of madness.
The music of amour is a confection,
And candy is reserved for the clouds.
Take heart before you break a heart
In your traveling road show of guile,
And leave her to languish with Lucifer!
There is no music in hell!

- Joanne de Simone

(Unyielding)

Thread color of siblings
In search of an obvious love
I did recognize a level of connect
To the spiritual given
It's the life given to us
Now that it belongs to us
A see through pleasure full mocking
The bending of the unyielding
Metric conversion

- Haim Mizrahi

THINGS

Keep the sparkly rings on your fingers,
As their lights are dim, offer no warmth—
Precious stones glimmer, but all that glitters
Come not from the truth that is Light.
Oh, Universe, generous with words found
In this Thesaurus pages between its covers,
Language offers comfort, wealth of knowledge,
Keeps the beauty of gliding ink guiding its path—
But no greater light, no greater warmth
Compares to the hospitality of the Sun.
Watch it rise—imagine the new day.
See it set—takes your breath away.
Reflect on it—hear the sound of love.
Language is only lavish when it is shared—
Shared with nature and the fertile mind
That creates, but cannot ever capture
The perfection of the Light.

- Joanne de Simone

$\mathcal{S}$uccumb

PLACE TO REST MY HEAD
AHEAD OF THE LIMITED EXPLANATION I WAS GIVEN
Tall smooth movement of progress
Suggesting the best route to be taken
To The one of a kind performance
As I was just about to witness
Every moment of shedding the enlightened
Telegraphing a swell move from another era
Of hidden desires bathing in their own balanced
Ability to size a moment of spiritual worthiness
That spells placing a dream
By way of creating from scratch an inflated God
Observing playfully already forgiving
The awkward movements of all The gathering well wishers
To the moon of personality and back to the enrollment
Of awareness to typically achieve
An acknowledgment of pretty face blending
In the crowd of that which averages a common look
Staring back in and zoom in the fashion it was touched
Being instructed to flash back the company
Of grip and succumb

- Haim Mizrahi

HEART MILES

Is it the geography that dictates desire,
Or the desire that allows the space to narrow?
Are the miles as important as the moments
That are shared after the miles are traveled?
From home to the horizon, I hear your heart—
Softly at first, from the long distance...then
To the blaring of bugles as we come closer,
Crashing with craving as we touch, embrace—
Slashing the miles, shifting and adjusting
The geography to accommodate the desire.
Then...the steps are turned around, returned
To the worn out map of constant footsteps—
But, there is no space between true hearts.

- Joanne de Simone

Taking Being Impressed
With a Grain of Salt

Lower the lights of self esteem more than
Pointing the evolution with thick gloves of a challenge
Well broken in and handled with a good reason to find
A level of seriousness overstated Overused
No more pleading to stone Gods
No more Gods erected
No mere More sense to the offerings
Lower your voice let the other voices
Agree with your tendency to Utilize
A room for even more reason and
Call for action city play engage lift
Observe level like mention
Adore
Respect
Cherish
Protect
Elevate
Show
Share
Shower
Shape
Point direct enrich describe favor
Mention regard type turn tell time
Taste trip trap top mention

To discover and what a moment
Offer deliberately and not more than
A huge mention in a form
Of a whisper of joint forces working for You
For me for your verse and feelings of amazement

- Haim Mizrahi

MEASURING UP

In the matter of the measurement,
It matters not the measure
Nor the magnitude,
But a mere manual manipulation
To determine a possible modification
To make a matchless match...
A flawless fit, as I recall,
With no maneuvers made at all.

- Joanne de Simone

$\mathcal{B}$iting The Air

We did the outmost of self absorbing
Talent and squeeze tactics
Of promises to be broken before the yield
Of guarding the somber briefer
You continue there we will catch up later on
I will then inform you of your passing away
Don't be surprised if you will not be able to answer me
After all the mouth of the hungry makes the gesture
Of biting the air that finds refuge in the free flowing nature
Substances to be spread and available
If only the needy will have the bit to offer in return
For the nothingness which hovers
Over the fake move of the super power
And I am impressed Nonetheless

- Haim Mizrahi

Second Harvest

Gone the days of early Spring
When our bones were new and strong
And stable and running miles and miles...
When we covered our dolls to keep them warm
And served them tea they could not drink...
When minds were sponges but we did not think—
When our reasoning was racing to catch up
With the boiling hormones of our bodies—
What have we learned from the flesh
And cells that withered with time?
Perhaps the Divine will grant us
A Second Harvest to help us, remind us
That along the way, we did, indeed
Win that elusive lottery once or twice—
And our senses responded, but...
It was too fleeting to remember!

- Joanne de Simone

erform

The point of the hazard sting of rubbing chin
Over an unknown gravity to Show the wait through
The self inflicted pain what a smile I detected
All the fumes of bullseye hit and run and regret
And show up and admit and pay the price
Love of after through a rhythm of mind blend
Spend trend shed so far into the awaiting
Twin feeling and unparalleled appearance
Thanks to you the executioner
The desk is wet destiny performs magnificently
So magnifying my love for you
At once many encounters of pride
With courage and fear for a lone stars burial

- Haim Mizrahi

ROBE

Under the ground, within the particles
Of dirt and worms, we probe for some use—
Something worthy, lasting...
The granules become rain-soaked,
And lose their relative substance,
So we must probe into the minuscule specks
To find life—not a symbol of death cocooned!
A green bud emerges—life! We delight
In probing the tiny leaf, the lasting sign
That it will survive the dirt blowing around,
Leaving us to probe deeper, deeper,
For a sign of life is precious to hold—to love.
The dirt of the earth must have meaning formed
From its former self to continue to survive!

- Joanne de Simone

And Strength

And you thought of the whereabouts
Crowd of manners let alone a spirit
Of Joint efforts were signals to me
The timing of great bearings
Sleeping through the wrinkles as it is
Creating an immediate looseness
The strength of hope and a constant maintenance

- Haim Mizrahi

How about we do...

How about we do
What we ought to do...
Maybe we can learn to lose
Ourselves in others' needs,
To bring us to a higher cause,
'Cause that will fill our souls.
How about we do
More of this when I write
With more than two hours sleep?
The muse is yawning...

- Joanne de Simone

Grinning

I love the idea of leaning
A small part in the pleading
Remark and star gaze feeling
Many of the slow motion peelings
Soft and scrub plenty of reading
Guide guise guise guide splitting
Point to the heart of admitting
Grand slopes nearby a silent hill

- Haim Mizrahi

$\mathcal{J}$UST ABOUT ANYTHING

Just about anything we do holds a value in time,
Though forgotten with the forward motion
Of the clock—tick...tick.
Just about anything and everything—but plastic
Has its reason to entreat and invite
Us to invent, to invest,
Knowing well that just about anything will end
In a single beat of the constant clock—tick...tick.
We are here to soak up just about anything,
Always hoping that some forward mobility
Will escape the tick...tick of the clock.

- Joanne de Simone

Depth of an old age

The floating refuge it's not known for being a safe heaven
Or at least being one who recognizes a freak show randomly
The lift was easy and swift it was not a struggle as was anticipated
Turning on a nail of heavily loaded flat bed on Godlike surfaces
I turn to you this time I greet you with a new apologetic demeanor
You were all the spell of late explosions of lust and pure love
Driven still in the depth of old age and forgetfulness
It was not a prey of any kind scent was not a cry out
Soon if haven't been a slow pride running long perusing itself
As if a burn followed by baby's teeth seeking the gratification
It belongs strictly to youth the thing in the early stages of release

- Haim Mizrahi

ASTEL-ISH

With the intention and extension
Of a friendly smile, an olive branch in hand,
But the symbol is in the shape of crayons,
Colored in aqua and lilac and pink...
The tones that will make a good heart think
That pastels in our lives lift the soul,
Erase the darkness—keep the soft greens,
Hold on while the deep purple weans
From the Chakras and opens doors...
Drop it, mash the black, stomp the floor.
Pastel-ish loves the light, holds the sight
Of goodness—all the days and all the nights.
Pastel-sh—beauty and light to adore,
Now, tomorrow and evermore.

- Joanne de Simone

The letter writer

Tremble in the course of a flexible
Mind to the matter of an inner invasion
You must be of age to cross the barrier
Of melting pots of finding out the pallets
Of the future a consumption of spiritual
Foods let alone the ringing of good will
Forming as they gain speed going down the avenue
You are all alone in this chapter ending action
Tell the letter writer of your love and yielding
So it can be written about anger and dismay instead
Appeasements flourishing in the confusion

- Haim Mizrahi

$\mathcal{H}$ALLOWEEN EVE

Here the living on Halloween
Look at Death straight on
In hideous costumes,
Mocking them on the other side,
As if we know the secret of life,
The possibility to stay here forever.
But those ghosts, how they laugh
At our arrogance and ignorance...
For an instant we shed the coils
That bind us to the still breathing
And become transparent souls,
Cold, but knowing that the warm blood
Of the living will drain anon,
And forever, as ghosts...Death remains.

- Joanne de Simone

ive Lines

Four five one three two
Two one four five three
One five four three two
Three two four five one
One three five two four

- Haim Mizrahi

DEAD FLOWERS

The flowers have died in short order,
Just like their season on earth—
Other gifts of material nature
Have diminished, shrunk in worth.
What remains is the reminder that
Death is always lurking in a corner,
Ready to snatch your joy in an instant—
His game is vile, jealous, cold, heady!
Hold on to the truth that is love.
No frills, no dressing, stark naked,
Kept warm by God's light all around.

- Joanne de Simone

Heat then melts

Traveling through the seeking Power
Time to load the challenge
As humility presents a leaf a feather
A smoothie Of some emotions still in search
Commonality and sameness of lord all mighty
We know the rest of the stretching stands fairly impressed
The other end welcomes the familiar self
From within the same self
Though a great deal of transformations took place
As the attempt to identify a feature of humanity
Running freely down cheek bones high
You are suddenly The top flare fire you never wither
Thinking of the heat then melts in a Proper fashion
Lord oh lord Temper fully scented going for the ultimate reaction
With full power disproportionate To the reaction
Therefore we are having lunch now
To think To think hard and well and loving

- Haim Mizrahi

HE'S ALIVE

His eyes never pass a flower blooming...
His ears can still hear the music...
His nose follows perfume that awakens...
His hands feel soft flesh in sweet love.

He tastes the wine, the vintage no matter...
Happy is he that is still alive and thrives..
Who knows not how his senses work,
And declares gratitude for the secret gifts.

In his anointed ignorance, he believes...
He's alive! He's alive!
Blessed breath that moves the heart...
He's alive! He's alive!

- Joanne de Simone

I for you

Pledge and I will make that strange Face
That you like so much
I love to see you amused happy
With your little moments working Respirator
Performing miracles to tribal people
Whom just came out of the cave of glory
I for you am for you hands on chest
Pride and an intimate exchange
knowing the contents a full package
Never to be opened
The rim shot squares loss of trapped ideas
And latching on to the first passerby
Merry merry on their way to the elements
The occurrences as being anticipated
By those who recall a different yesterday

- Haim Mizrahi

*E*h!

Eh! He uses cell phones as he drives,
For years he's gone unnoticed
Until the cop pulls him over!
Eh! I finally got caught, he thinks,
But why not just a warning
Since I was in a state of distress?
Eh! The cop has to do his job,
His quota he must fill.
Go chase the goddamned drug lords
And the shooters in the square.
Eh! It's just a phone on my ear.
I drive very well with one hand.
The cop writes him up—
And he's..."Eh! I hate cops!"
Lesson not learned.
Eh!

- Joanne de Simone

# Five sixths

Tree ok my lowest expectation
Soft on the light side of The spirit
Spearheading a glory of other casualties
gone to the pit of rot and soft disappearance
Losing track

- Haim Mizrahi

A WEDGE ON THE LEDGE

Round is the earth,
But on it a ledge...
Find the wedge,
Dig in your heel,
Lean on the wall...
We can still fall
After killing it all.
The wedge will fill,
Earth cured of the ill,
While out on the ledge
cramped in the grooved wedge...
The round earth spins still.

- Joanne de Simone

The distance

Tap tap tap you are there freshly soaked
Level nose breathing tapestry learn nine
Circles slur and speech was key
How is it about to glide with invalid tools
Slam party after the hours of precious investments
Humming a greeting of roots coated with charm marbles
To a first time realtor offers a jewel planing the roast
Or out of season outdoor activity shaming the visitor
To the main slow clock over the instruction of handing the helm
Before the squick of Voice warm safe
Playing the distance of no distance

- Haim Mizrahi

ℛEMOTE

Remote is a gadget
With a battery included.
Remote is depression
When the battery is low.
Remote is a place
Where nature is heard.
Remote is somewhere
Where footsteps are rare.
Remote is the open air
Where the sky is vast.
Remote is the Universe
Where minds ascend.
Remote never defines love
When batteries are included.

- Joanne de Simone

$\mathcal{H}$eat

Sweet paradise love is in the air
As your cheeks
Present the blush of the world
Kneeling alongside your shadow
What a relief
You're scent lifting my thoughts
Through the bushes of natural growth
I love you with my eyelashes flattering your
Presence for ever dream like presence full of the memories
And Aging without The fear holding on to your love for me...
With my life with my admiration for your intellectual heat
Those cheeks of yours
Lift me Up to the shoulder line of your beauty

- Haim Mizrahi

Studio

She stands on a platform
And she is scrutinized...
The artist is at home,
Pulling her attributes
From every angle...
The light changes
As the sun moves—
How different her form
When the shadow embraces
Her round uncovered curves...
The artist in his habitat
Holds the pallette
That holds the colors
To capture
The light and shade
Of his glorious subject...
The place is designed for it.

- Joanne de Simone

Shelter

I slowed down since I
Realized how much I desire you
Especially knowing you Will never be mine
But mine you are nevertheless
Loose ends Brushing The challenge
The order Of things in this forest
I shelter My weakness inside the tree stems
Eyeing The progress of your heart beat beat beat
And I slow down since it's the affair of loving everywhere

- Haim Mizrahi

Not an Issue Anymore

Perfunctory tidings
In place of love proclaimed—
Not an issue anymore.
Adjusted to the absence
Of your smiles, expressions—
Not an issue anymore.
To see behind the mask
Or into your bag of tricks
Wondering what is real—
Not an issue anymore.
Freedom to breathe
To seek deeper passion
In a world beyond you—
Not an issue any more.
Or is it?

- Joanne de Simone

$\mathcal{S}$pread Sheet

Pray slowly
Makeshift statue of the look of sanctity
Evolve a rain drop
Not wet enough for agriculture
Drain pipe of foreign prospects
Spreadsheet of melodies
So quietly serving the picture perfect hum
To the nights Of pronounced partings
As it must end without an incident

- Haim Mizrahi

THROUGH THE DOOR

Step on the floor, go through the door,
A new door, not entered before...
The walls are painted white and plain,
But there's a crack in the wall
That calls to you...
Its imperfection will find
Its own redemption
Through your inspiration,
As it is a reflection
Of your motivation...
Perhaps the shadows and light
Are the shades of your soul,
Half or whole...
Paint it! Write it! Create it!
Its flaw is the magic you find
When you step on the floor
And walk through a new door...

- Joanne de Simone

h Boy

Baby you are a baby boy
Oh boy you are a baby forever
In the realm of crawling
Like a baby boy girl
You are a baby so baby like
You are a sweet baby
Like the moon
A Resting position
And a real time
First steps of tears
Anticipating a roar of gentleness
And promises for firm walks through the slow movements
Grandpa is trying to close the gaps
And give you the biggest kiss in the world
Because you are his baby

- Haim Mizrahi

CRUISING THE ROUGH SEAS

These are the times when the waves are high,
The seas are rough, white caps a blanket...
The sea is a watery boundary,
Keeping us from touch.
The water is not kind...
Drowns our hearts.
The boat cruises, bounces,
Seeks in vain
The warmth, the love...
They're going under.
No hand reaches out,
Recoiling in fear...
Touching is prohibited
In the rough sea.
We need find our way alone
From a distance,
Keeping our distance.
But, oh, the longing
To hold one another...
To calm the rough sea,
A sea of loneliness.
We shall weep with joy
At first embrace
When the storm passes...
We shall revel in the fervor
And the calm of skin on skin.

- Joanne de Simone

$\mathcal{P}$lot Beggar

A tribe of slur of lust duration in abundance
A gifted old man looking to add a puzzle revelation
Present shout archive plot beggar alive attributed haul
It has worked into level dark swing up hill pledge
And with an exhaling heart hard harsh having hosting
Hives Hilling has had have heard hush hearing
Home heartedly Hose high here harmony hip
Heap hip heat hit heap hiss holy hard has hairy hail hove host
Hostile here hold hear Hardly hypnosis hearsay hot hall
Heave hazard hold host Harry

- Haim Mizrahi

$\mathcal{A}$ PROPER POEM

Asked to write a proper poem...
First ask what is proper.
Does it satisfy the lonely heart?
Will it catch the reader from the start?
A proper poem has rhythm or rhyme,
Becomes a song with music in time...
No! Its definition sets the rule,
But robs the artist his craft and tool.
Write a proper poem, he said...
I'll try like a mule to be lead,
Though the Proper is an insult
To all who beg for the unusual muse.

- Joanne de Simone

Harry

Heart hard harsh having hosting hives
Hilling has had have heard
Hush hearing home heartedly
Hose high here harmony
Hip heap
Hip heat hit
Heap hiss
Holy hard has hairy hail
hove host hostile here hold hear
Hardly hypnosis hearsay
Hot hall heave hazard
Hold host harry

- Haim Mizrahi

$\mathcal{I}$ WENT TO BED AT 3 O'CLOCK

The night fell hours before,
The moon set, sun on the green.
At three o'clock I am in bed,
Flat, awake, eyes fairly bulging.
Entreating the Sandman to shut them,
To dream a wish fulfillment...
I went to bed at three o'clock
With a mind packed with politics,
The ramming voices of radio rhetoric.
Comfort has not come, hope...perhaps.
At three o'clock, I am sullen, frozen...
Sleep come soon! I need my mind
To write this with its title yet unknown.

- Joanne de Simone

$\mathcal{S}$urety

Tempered arm raised to be rich and generous
Sorting a hound celebration
The lungs of breathing afterwards a signal travels
A bit slow motion on dark lightened roll over
Visit of promising friendship of strangers measuring
The given word of shelter symbol of trust and assurances
As softening of climbing hills of slide surety to a childhood
Remaining somewhat for teaching lessons in the near future not
so near

- Haim Mizrahi

3 O'CLOCK IN THE AFTERNOON

Three o'clock states the clock...
Had your lunch, just because
The music left me at noon
After teasing me with words
That do not rhyme, offer no reason
Since seven this morning!
Three o'clock—
Evening on the way,
With nothing worthy yet to say...
Maybe the message will remain gray
Until the words will find meaning
When stuck together on the page.

- Joanne de Simone

$\mathcal{F}$orty Four

Father flow fur fast folly firm
Fashion for first feast fan frosting flash
Free Free free rather for four forty four
Fasting first foraging forest fathers
Free for fraction film first father flow fiction forehead

- Haim Mizrahi

No TIME, NO SLEEP

In the abyss, the tunnel
Of exhaustion, no light...
No twinkle of a single star,
Without inspiration
From the past or
Motivation from the future...
Standing still, seeking words,
Fatigue is your fanciful friend,
Or your enemy, whatever he be,
Positioned, with the muse
His hostage until
He allows the creation
To come alive...
In the middle of no time,
No sleep.

- Joanne de Simone

*P*ull Go Guts

It's a zoom practice the invite of an end of line impatience
A limit of late night shopping not supposing to be there
To begin with pull pull pull you sob
A grabber of garbage gearing go guts explosion
Yet you are me hiding in a flow of disabilities
So full of capabilities theirs to celebrate
Her in me gorging deaf an unbearable beauty

- Haim Mizrahi

THE SLEEP SHIFT

Shifting sleep lie in
The graveyard shift...
For people who dream by day.
Is the clock our guide
Or reminder to give
It all a rest...to shift?
Do stones sleep in a quarry?
Does the sun awaken a stone?
Set your clock to the tick-tock
Of your creative heart—
Not the rock...
Shift your human energy
As nothing is written in stone.
We just feel it more keenly.
Why? I never asked a stone.

- Joanne de Simone

Glide a Touch

Oh dear in the wetness of walking sliding sliding
The walls of a horizon glide touch the need of mine
To bring to you the happy relief of belonging
Hushly to preserve a sing along the need of generations
Neglect and forbidding the entrance of weakness
Confessions oh dear love of hidden admiration
Yours the portion which belongs to me dive a hill climb
And then descends a portion of reality to open the gates
To thrive between your arms

- Haim Mizrahi

IMPRESSED

Taking being impressed with a grain of salt—
Lot's wife became a pillar of salt.
Was she too impressed with being?
Being impresses is against the nature of being,
As being as One is what impresses—
One with the colors of the mismatched skies
That give each place an honest hue
Blended with all it covers—
Being impressed with man's hand
Is not impressive.
It deserves the sprinkle and grains.
It is a collective gratefulness for
Nature's wonders.
That it is all taken with a grain of salt—
That is the blindness—that is the sin!
It is unforgivable to pass a flower
And to be not impressed by its beauty,
And to take it with a grain of salt.

- Joanne de Simone

Sour Bitter

And me hand in hand play the rule of tempting
And to be a non participating participator
A part Of innocence for the mass options
Frees suggestions taking me to the realization
You fool how could you have been pulled
Into momentary pleasure not yours
Forbidden sweet sour bitter
Better than a crunchy breakfast prepared by strangers
For strangers how strange to learn and utilize
And remember and elevate as a whole

- Haim Mizrahi

DOES THE PETAL KNOW?

Does the petal know it is doomed?
Is the stem shivering as it climbs?
The leaves brown from no mist?
So proud it stands, face to the sky,
Innocent of its fate.
Is it really given a fair shot?
A part-time lover cuts it down
To give it to an unworthy maiden
Just to make her smile for an instant?
Poor lady, with her sad occupation
To watch the slow shrinking of petals,
As death comes to the flower...
Before its time.

- Joanne de Simone

The Equipment

Same time same place
Don't know what it means
Don't know what to make of it
It's dragging it's not it's playing me it's not
It's loving me it's not
It's helping me it's not
It's enlightening forgiving and tailing
The slur of perfection
Interested to affect
The grave digger of birth
First I spite a time to return the equipment
And thank the manufacturer
For a great ride short

- Haim Mizrahi

SPEAK OF THE DEVIL

Speak of the Devil,
Put his name on a blank sheet
And see the dark of his soul
Lost in Hades.
Let him stay, give him not
His filthy song on air waves.
Diminish his power with silence.
Slam the door.
Watch him shrink, shrivel
At the sound of love and joy,
At the colors of a wheel of worth,
As we walk away from the Devil
We alone created.
Speak not his name.
Write not his letters.
Paint not his face.
Tear the sheet.
Drop the brush.
He is not there!

- Joanne de Simone

I want to forget to remember

Forget about it
What? What?
What?
What? What? What? What?
What?
What?
What? What? Wheat?
What?
Oh ok yes I remember

- Haim Mizrahi

SHALL WE SAY WHAT

Shall we say what is the next move
To the purpose of our plight?
Shall we question the past
As to the rhythm of the future?
With no strings or broken keys
Playing out of time all our life?
Shall we say what is discarded
In our conscious minds to leave
For the nobility and beauty?
Shall we just say Screw It,
And be the river's rock,
Standing, waiting for the slam
Of the waters? Why not?

- Joanne de Simone

$\mathscr{F}$ree Cruise Grain

Prefer not the option of side rhythms
Then missing the beauty
Yet accurate meetings
Taking the place of late encounters
With supposedly an offer to eloquently
Prematurely fly the skies with wings
And extreme ability to impress self
And then the improper location and options at
Your disposal getting the hints while advancing
To use a ladder of high risk and travel against the grain
Elevations strike free cruise
In the unforgiving skies yours now for the duration

- Haim Mizrahi

EOGRAPHY

Is it the geography that dictates desire,
Or the desire that allows the space to narrow?
Are the miles as important as the moments
That are shared after the miles are met?
From across those long miles
I can hear your heart...
Softly, first, at the long distance,
Then blaring as we come closer,
Crashing with craving as we touch...
Slashing the miles, shifting, adjusting
The geography, accommodating the desire.
There is no space between true hearts.

- Joanne de Simone

Gross Trust

Real digging in the nights of short hopes
Sparks of doubts and memories of loved ones
They are dear and locked into the fear
End of life approaching no no no
The time is out of reach digging in
The new answer Oh sweat flourish
Purpose temple of man worshiping man
Gross trust of Tunnel caving in
And imminent collapse Probing limitlessly
Aspirations of approaching Easements
Unprepared yet eager to end the story at any cost

- Haim Mizrahi

WITHOUT MUSIC

Without music, on the spot...
No notes to give life
To these lines of no meaning.
Without music, the words
Just go flat to the ground.
No discovery.
Without music, it's just letters
From a pen, jumbles...
No beginning, a premature end.

- Joanne de Simone

$\mathcal{N}$othing comes

Comes to come to me
Best of happy companions
Come come you can allow
The dry tears to express
Thought irrigation come
Nothing harm will come your way
Leased to a new travel stream streak
Lowering expectations in the height
Of less accountable promise breaks
Come and go nothing comes

- Haim Mizrahi

THE POSITIVE ASPECT OF TEMPER

Face the wrath, bring it on!
It cannot penetrate.
Your shield is the positive
Aspect of temper.
Which tempers your temper
When the knives are drawn.
Your light surrounds you—
It creates a tempered temper
That smiles, accepts
Only good, only noble.
All aspects of love
Will temper the beast of anger.
You are safe in the positive...
The negative dissolves
At the powered Divine.

- Joanne de Simone

Learn to appeal to personal pairs...

- H. M.

$\mathcal{S}$pace

Leverage leverage leverage leverage leverage
Leverage leverage leverage
Leverage
Leverage leverage
Leverage leverage leverage
Leverage
Leverage leverage leverage leverage
Leverage
Leverage leverage
Leverage leverage leverage
Leverage leverage
Leverage leverage leverage leverage leverage leverage

- Haim Mizrahi

A SHORT ONE

Have a short one?
Make mine a double.
Too much clutter...
Needs to be swept.
A short one would
Not end the trouble.
Make mine a double.

- Joanne de Simone

$\mathcal{T}$wo lines

You grab the cannot as it reveals a power
To change all that which does not exist

- Haim Mizrahi

$\mathscr{T}$HE BIRD IN THE SKY

Let it go, watch it fly...
Beautiful bird
With no worries
High in the sky...
When you fly low
And if I look up
And praise your charm...
You shit in my eye!

- Joanne de Simone

$\mathcal{D}$istribution

IT'S NO LONGER A RIDGE of jumping over thoughts
It's a reality within its promises to its carrying vessel
A dream comes true leisure travel lifting a note
To the blazing king in the moment of pleasure
Issuing proclaiming downward motions
Restrictions erected in times of externalizing
Its potential love a distribution its normal I was told
it's wet and slippery and clean and clear
It's a winning proposition feasting at ease
Wishing the moment of grabbing our lives
From its placement reaching a grip of abnormality

- Haim Mizrahi

PILING UP

Thoughts circling, nonsense tossed in storms—
Piling up.
Words unsaid, muted by fear—
Piling up.
Art, dried paint on pallets—
Piling up.
Poems, letters on ladders—
Piling up.
The past, the now, the future—
Smashed in a pile-up.
Purge the phrases, the thoughts and dreams,
Let them die in the pile-up
In the weary arms of the Muse.
Let them all fall.
Clear the road—
End the piling up.

- Joanne de Simone

O'clock

Three o'clock actually it's three fifteen
And the difference splits between the task at hand
And the desire to hide behind the sleepy world
One wall two walls three walls forth is missing
Temporary self standing structure hovering over my
Desire to bypass the elements of dispersed matter
And a realization it's mine outside of me around me
And I stare at it I am good at staring
I am a big stare looking deeply inside the questions
As wishful thinking forming alongside my knowledge
Of the feelings of belittlement Approaching three thirty five

- Haim Mizrahi

FIVE LINES

Turn off the phone and TV,
Listen to music, sway.
Close the book, stretch...
Turn to your lover
With a passionate look!

- Joanne de Simone

Mornings reminders

Left to encounter the numbers with passion
The shadow appears to disappear
And the shadow Has a purpose
Lifting the attention above the time set to three o'clock
Posing for a morning's reminder
You came from here through there
Wishing the loophole of forgetfulness
He is there in waiting I heard the voice announcing
I realized it was me dreaming of my success
I am showing others the way to the gates of sleep

- Haim Mizrahi

POETRY IS THE CROWN OF THE PASSAGE (don't use the work 'bridge')

Without the word, how can I describe you?
Interim passage between the lovers?
He stands on one side, indifferent,
The unknown kiss awaits in shadows.
You are the word I cannot use.
Your are the footing holding me up,
Away from troubled waters below.
If I choose to take that route, that is,
To heal, find someone real.
You are not real...
You are that forbidden word
Holding me up while I cross over,
Keeping me safe?
Fine, I guess...
It's freeing.
It's life.
We take the journeys
We cross the...
To find new life.
You can lead me there.
No harm, right?

- Joanne de Simone

Shy movements

You heard yourself you are moving you are surrounded
You are a fraction of innocent attempts to close in tight
You are not sure you are ready
You are not certain You are a part of it
You mend and glue and press together from above
The light is not working any longer
Yet the shine of search is unbearable tic Toc tic toc

- Haim Mizrahi

GENEROSITY OF LANGUAGE FROM THE UNIVERSE

Keep the sparkly rings on your fingers,
As their lights are dim, and offer no warmth—
Precious stones glimmer but all that glitters
Came not from the true world of Light.
Oh, Universe, generous with words
Found in thick Thesaurus pages between its covers,
Language offers comfort, wealth of knowledge,
Keeps the beauty of ink to guide the path—
But no greater light, no cocooned warmth
Compares to the hospitality of the Sun.
Watch it rise—imagine the new day.
Watch it set—takes your breath away.
Language is only generous when it is shared
With nature and a fertile mind that creates
But cannot capture the perfection of Light...
Even with the generosity of language from the Universe.

- Joanne de Simone

rotest

The vessel of preoccupation now is present
I it with high regard rolling with my presumption to empty
A rocking chair with contents never seen before
Rock you rocky rocking rock sweet turn spindle of sugar
Melted in the form of protest and shining melt
Glaze on culinary promise and dance gaily
You wonder no longer you wonder
You open the split decision
To keep on wondering a single promise
To spectators par excellence

- Haim Mizrahi

WHISPERS

Whispers are loud they curse
The words tossed in foolishness.
Laptops, emails, texts...all social
But not socially agreeable.
A coward types and tweets,
But to your face he'll smile,
Whisper his hate, perhaps,
And it will still grate
On the soul of the Universe—
Upend it with feces chatter.
Use the whisper or shout it out.
Turn your heart to love,
And whispers become Divine
Crashing cymbals and drums.

- Joanne de Simone

*M*ight money

One and two and add no more
I left early this morning with a roar
Draining posture straight and firm
Post embankments with a yearn
Might you hold the anchor safe
I prefer the look alike face
Pray to the familiar fit of reckon
You are back now for eggs and bacon
Sleep over better for your tired eyes
Please remind me of what money buys

- Haim Mizrahi

$\mathcal{S}$O I THINK IT'S TIME

So I think it's time to shake
The leaves and bare the branches—
Maybe the tree will weave...
Maybe its roots are not deep.
I think it's time to strip the bark
Naked, vulnerable to the core...
It cannot hide, the view is wide—
All around through light and dark...
I think it's time to see it all—
The love, the hate, the glass wall...
Maybe it's not a tree at all.
Maybe it's a thin twig, easily snapped—
I think it's time to let it snap...
To let it die, brittle on the ground—
I think it's time to step and to go
And plant a new one...
So, as we reap, so will we sow.

- Joanne de Simone

Remote

Deeper into the session of lavish chain of thoughts
Love to sit and chat within an aspect of dry mouth and a
crunchy ear
Lower your voice the sound of soft and mentioned to the
crackforming
Speaking of a leverage to switch the contents of sobriety
Heal kneel breathe right turn all the way against the agility and
being soft spoken
Behind the closet without any room to hide relieved for the
exposure
To find a brink without a leap to watch for

- Haim Mizrahi

$\mathcal{C}$OLOR

Conqueror of my heart as it beats,
Only beating to survive without
Love to pump it with desire...
Over you...my injured soul, too.
Ruptured from your slow cuts and splinters.

- Joanne de Simone

$\mathcal{H}$ousing colors

Studio mine left behind
Studio serves to remind
Have a real edge of patching
Mentioning the role of watching
Noticed scene of formula
Against the odds of I don't know ya
Left to fend for the pigments
Out of sessions for regiments
Leak of smiles at ease
Let me in please

- Haim Mizrahi

WE DID THAT ALREADY

We did that already.
We colored inside the lines.
We made an attempt
To make the line finer—
The colors inside more vital,
More alluring in the day,
As the sun made our efforts easy.
But at night, in the dark,
When faith is all there is,
The colors fade, darken...
Your scent drifts into the air.
The lines are blurred.
We did that already.
Always the same refrain—
All the colors blended, muddied...
Too much effort to try again
What we already did.

- Joanne de Simone

Dig

Issue the terms not anymore a factor
To land and pick the debris of meaning
All over the sidewalks of a flattened repent
Against a beauty travel plans and an uncontrollable
Entity in your face telling you your days are numbered
I love numbers but not when it comes to counting down
The days of my existence on planet earth dig

- Haim Mizrahi

Boom!

Boom! There it goes—gone!
All we need to survive
On this earth was in the earth.
Nature gifted us the care
And the cure for all the ills.
Boom! How smug we became!
What hubris to steal a leaf,
Mix with water, stir Big Pharma
Who takes the credit.
Earth, Herself, nurse and healer
Knew it all...had it all!
Boom! We are the killers of cures.

- Joanne de Simone

Submission

Roach of illusions pretty face of matter melt
Pride half looks observe dead ends meetings
Lets the slow advance preach with secrecy
Now turn the red cheek now blow the air
Stale and short center thriving with quiet observations
Is it known by now the call for order
Wrecking down the place of worship

- Haim Mizrahi

Nature Being Nature

The rocks in the calm sea
Our feet walk upon
Are easy to tread...
Find a pebble in your shoe—
It aches, cuts, causes woe.
Add a leak from the ceiling,
Maddening as we sleep.
Nature is a soothing woman—
She can also be a Bitch!

- Joanne de Simone

$\mathcal{U}$ntitled

To a registered well wishers
Between the lowering
Expectations without a good reason
Back door thrives welcome

- Haim Mizrahi

I'M GOING TO PLAY THE DRUMS FOR FIVE MINUTES

Taking five! Picking up the sticks!
Fill the air with thunder.
The beat unsteady,
But ready to shake the floor.
Taking five! Picking up the sticks!
Beating a few tricks
To beat the storm
That rolls in my mind.
Be kind to the sticks!
They control the beat—
Even for only five minutes!

- Joanne de Simone

I want to write

Your writing sucks because I never red a book in my life
Your writing Is wholesome it makes me hungry is it a good thing
Or maybe it's a way to bring myself closer to tell you I love you
I wrote something once it said I want to write so I can look with stillness into
The horizon but nothing much of the anticipated magic of the horizon materialized
But all of that being said it still does not make your writing any better...

Love of progress team of fans party

- Haim Mizrahi

FREE VERSE

The verse is free,
Pen to paper,
Able to bring
Thoughts to paper...

Free is the verse
Of our own lives,
Speak in the open,
Stifle not the words...

If pen can move
Without limitation
And paper is willing
To accept all manner...

Then we of flesh
With air ever fresh
Shall be as free
As pen and its paper.

- Joanne de Simone

$\mathcal{H}$anging Bloom

Left home early
Green thought barely
Liking the bloom
Praying for a groom
Rich in the shadow
Left to playdow
Prince of the deserved
Hanging high and observed
I reached another home
As I was pronged
Not even a wink
Served as a link
To whom addressed the hymns
I lowered my voice with pins
Love to chat longer
Though getting away feels stronger
Till next time
When I am in my prime

- Haim Mizrahi

*I*T

It's time to look at the root,
The root of the trees
Planted those years ago.
It was a tree of freedom,
But its roots have rotted,
Drowned the earth in hate.
If it can stand strong,
If justice prevails,
It can live forever.
If it's seen as a monument
Of love an care,
It's branches grow high
In the sky, always green,
Ever green, our tree,
Surviving forever
From roots newly natured.

- Joanne de Simone

$\mathcal{A}$ bundle of goodness

Not long not short not happy not grumpy
I admire reaching out I like you for a moment
I looked hard the other day I was so close
But questions appeared in the kind of logic they like to present
Love of self so crucial to push away the trouble makers
Sing along pretty face must you complain about beauty
As you carry your majestic looks around I give this to you
You are a bundle of goodness wrapped with joy
You cannot show or expression but I know
Because I know and let's leave it at that

- Haim Mizrahi

$\mathcal{D}$UST

From dust we can, to dust return...
And so it ends, and so we end...
It's fate.
Our time here, much dust gathered
On our soles, in our souls.
Kick it off shoes, walk fast—
Particles swell, blocking the way...
Muddled thoughts, those dusty days.
Trick the mind, that tricky dust.
Walk it off...it follows us—
Leaving life's unfinished footprints.
Hidden dust corrodes our souls,
Brings us back again for a purer run—
Another turn to make art of the dust,
But in the end, it's all just dust.

- Joanne de Simone

Cleaning up the path ahead of us...

- H. M.

Ideas of affections

In Silence I greet you my beloved
You must think I love sparingly without surety
But not so fast buster, I don't know what made me say that
Anyway I love you nicely with juices to spare can you relate
Never mind I think the world of you around you and me
Surrounding the ideas of affections telling the short stories
Of age long piles of history to be repeated
And maybe giving us a better hint on how to love more or less

- Haim Mizrahi

$\mathcal{S}$OLELY

Solely, surely, sensually, self-absorbed,
Sophomoric sensations start in youth—
Directed by nature as it surrounds us
Spiriting to perpetuate, regenerate, procreate—
Solely for our souls comes sacred sensations.
We seek, need, survive with the other, another.
Nothing is really solely—
All is an honored coupling—
As in a Shakespeare sonnet.

- Joanne de Simone

Mouth dripping

Temper of saving the word for a brighter cause
See the shade of that big humongous tree with the branch almost
falling
Well stay clear of the suggestive lines of nature's independence
Clear stream back yard lashing the silence into submission
The cries don't matter any longer the swallow of contempt
Becomes the anger in store for a new era to unfold
And Pick up the anger to new nights flow freely
Replays an eyelash in its passage of reluctance
Don't let the structure present an uneven fact of matter pilling
Clinging making sounds of anger anger
As beeps of termination a reminder of life strength depth death
Birth reevaluation to a brink of eyes open wide
And mouth dripping frozen mists

- Haim Mizrahi

Just Another One

Just another one
Because the pen is hot.
It sizzles with steamed ink,
Letters are aflame
As they slide down...
When words come together
On the cold page
Or on a plastic screen,
They cool off, freeze.
They huddle together
Only to survive
And only to make sense
Of just another one!

- Joanne de Simone

(Title)

Give way take treasure
Plead calm cover surge
Bleed red
Shed moisture
Lay heat on
Pray singing
Play birth
Smile completion
Walk forth
Back to life

- Haim Mizrahi

To FORGET

I want to forget to remember
That I filled a book
With silly phrases of
The pain of unrequited love,
When I had the chance to write
Of mutual affection, but turned
To insipid mournful words
That all who read, forgot!
I want the same privilege,
I want to forget to remember
The futile art of memory.
It serves not mind nor soul.

- Joanne de Simone

(ITLE)

A trip to heaven
Over the straight oath
Offerings for mighty plurals

- Haim Mizrahi

ASTEST POEM

Chris and Heather
Sped through the forest.
Chris was strong,
Grabbed all the food,
Ate Heather for lunch.

- Joanne de Simone

Covered

Laugh as northern stars gazing in the spiral fright
Prince of merger lasting proof pride covered
Begging the virtual sorting bigger than a love song
Pretty and sad heart of surge

- Haim Mizrahi

*I*F IT'S SOMETHING

If it's something
It came from nothing,
Though nothing comes—
It's spontaneous appearance.
Let the nothing that comes
Kill the No, keep the Thing—
It comes, it creates,
It becomes...something
Out of nothing that comes
From the fertile nothingness,
Which, of course, is rather something!

- Joanne de Simone

$\mathcal{I}$mpressive

Tight spot rich contents lifeless vital nevertheless
Leave it be it never conserved its energy for people to benefit
One legged crime chaser how I don't know
And impressive record
As a company of deference
For crime unfolding without interruption
There is a new sheriff in town
The wheelchair of justice is back

- Haim Mizrahi

$\mathscr{L}$EVERAGE

On the surface it can hold...
It can keep things straight.
We can stand and wait
For the balance that gives...
For the signs to live
With the pillars that hold
And to fortify existence...
It has a name, always there.
The average, the middle,
The leverage we keep...

- Joanne de Simone

$\mathcal{D}$rawling

Tried it a couple of times
I am drawling spiking a bystander
Though I cared for him
I could not show mercy
I apologize but you cannot hear my pain anymore
Tried it a couple of times
And not sure how to proceed

- Haim Mizrahi

$\mathcal{O}$N THE TRACK

On the track, in the groove,
But watch that groove...
It becomes deeper in time,
Too deep to escape.
On the track, off the groove,
Taking the journey...
Jumping the track
To unknown fields
To weeds or flowers
Bye-bye track,
Hello new road,
Or old road hat looks new
To fool us...no matter!
You have power to create
New, smooth invisible grooves—
And that is groovy!

- Joanne de Simone

Grip

Trauma pleasant the king is looking at the crowded crowd
I knew there was love out there for me
Maybe this time I am right
The backlash leaves tracks hard to remove
But who In his tight mind will try to remove them
A will engraved in the hard surface of chilling
When there is a good reason to
The atmosphere is well claimed and
The grip is a tight hold this time
Excuse me did you see my Incompetence
Traveling illegally against the traffic
Did you whisper with delight

- Haim Mizrahi

RAUMA

It comes on heavy feet
In the wake of the loss...
It's the drama without art,
It invades the peace.
It's name is Trauma.

- Joanne de Simone

Oh my

Taxi taxi shit taxi taxi taxi
Crap taxi oh taxi please taxi
Taxi taxi taxi shoot taxi
Oh my taxi taxi almost
Taxi taxi taxi taxi no no no no taxi
Taxi Taxi Taxi oh my oh my
This one was mine taxi

- Haim Mizrahi

TRENCHES

The artist's life is
One in a trench.
An artist can only toil
With the madness
He was given—
Compelled to stay
Scratching in the pit.
Pity the poor ignorant
With gift-wrapped rot.
They do not create—
Their hands are pink,
Absent ink and paint.
Their shoes polished
With unworn heels.
Come down, drone,
Into the trench and learn.

- Joanne de Simone

uch

A Visual brink an entrance
To an agile pain scenario
Last attempt ceasing to black out
With pretty face poaching
Light head sprinkle of shedding
Cover for a long drying time
Dress undress dream unleash
Learn remote fiction of love
Ouch ouch ouch ouch ouch

- Haim Mizrahi

$\mathcal{L}$URE

The black T-shirt has on its front
A single white triangle...
Its face-worn USA.
I am intrigued, lured ento learning
Of the warriors and their stories,
Lured, as they are from my country.
How many war stories
Fit in that chest-sized triangle?
Lure me in, speak to me—
Relieve me of the ignorance.
Enlighten me with new curiosity.
Lure me. Lure me.

- Joanne de Simone

$\mathcal{S}$ervice

Tryout the turn was missed missing the target
Salvation a ritual of forgiveness and therefore
A prince of charm runs a livid cause
And a remorse for making out later on
Low pitch in the service of muted requirements
And secured longevity to the assurance
Of going along passages of a pretty face
On its way to loosen its head literally

- Haim Mizrahi

IN OPPOSITION

To oppose the opposition
We are given a life in dreams,
Opposing the reality of
Wakefulness to oppose hunger—
In dreams, a feast,
Or more starvation
If the REM is too rough
To oppose the opposition
Of loves lost.
Our senses bring in both
In a more perfect form
To oppose the belief
Of a failed life.
Dreams expose us
In our work, our goal...
To oppose is to surrender
However it comes...

- Joanne de Simone

You Carry Me

Love to see you dance around the idea of freshness soul searching
You mean a lot to the tree hugger of your time
Note by note fright and weight not at risk of any delay
you are light on your feet
You carry me as you are not limited
Only the expression of the body
Grooves to display a call for help
Without the alarming cry

- Haim Mizrahi

THE PLASTIC BAG

The plastic bag that gripped your lunch
This time has a use.
The clock with numbers reminds us
To take the lunch, eat it.
The plastic bag may have a steady job
It deserves, as useful.
But, this time it goes in the ocean
To choke a harmless fish.
The clock keeps ticking...
The dust accumulates...
But it has its place, a steady job,
For this time, for time, for any time.

- Joanne de Simone

$\mathcal{I}$t carries

A day of sun an understanding of the anxious
Around the corner of a sunny day
Sunday a day with three sons and one lovely daughter
It Carries the intriguing feeling of togetherness
A trip to mama and papa
They are no longer here with us
Though Sunday remains a reminder of vacancy
Telling belongs to the history of the teller

- Haim Mizrahi

$\mathcal{B}$UBBLE

In this bubble
Being watched.
An artist waits
To see what spills
From this lonely quill—
What drops and flows
From the squishy mind.
The sweat spreads.
Mush! Mush!
Go, go, Yukon dog
Of a writer, rushed,
Pulled, pushed...
All at the dictionary's whim.

- Joanne de Simone

*B*e Beaver

Beaver was not in the room this time
A roll of dice in a private setting
Leaves the room before the storm
Which might leave you naked
This time beaver was an example
A portion of a cloture
A touch of the familiar
A home a neighborhood
A safe haven for a shifting responsibility
A Civil format of assumptions
A consequence so plenty

So what's it going to be beaver

- Haim Mizrahi

Taxi (remembering my father)

Taxi! Taxi!
He heard the call
For forty years and more.
My father, yes he did.
Pushed hack
Fourteen hours a day
On the night shift
In Manhattan,
On the streets.
Rolled drunks too blind
To see the meter.
Taxi! Taxi!
When the cabs were yellow
That roamed on avenues
That went both ways.
His only way to earn a buck.
Taxi! Taxi! He heard the call.
His own boss...best of all!

- Joanne de Simone

$\mathcal{A}$nd yourself

Now that they poured the oil to silk the process
To declare majestically you are on your own
A pretty sad fraction of wise cracks holding on to the grid
The sense of urgency to keep that heritage going
You and I and yourself so much more
Due to our entitlement recognition
We got each others back

- Haim Mizrahi

$\mathcal{I}$DEAS

Empty the mind, fill the mind.
Ideas...what are they?
Puffs of vapor that drift away
When another pushes hard.
Find the space, let it sit
With its own emerging light,
While ideas, those flaky notions
Work their way in and make
Your way to unchartered paths—
Towards what? Another idea?

- Joanne de Simone

# Freelance

Pearls shoot the breeze of wind.

Mmm the turn over blinks at night the shift of a royal skin
Posting the scent of mankind level three shrinking in a good Way
polite and eager to apply the knowledge of beast over
The lives of screen and portion of freelancing the scan as
Breathtaking pearls shoot the breeze of wind stride no left to Stray
in the gutter of fruit learn brace seasons brought
Partial beam strike heart of gold based blessed
The precious metal deep estimation breath in soulful of the
Country kind the foliage of identity marking of sweet tasty The
pride and all buds of regression brisk of tale livid
Branch extends oh pretty one to the deep soul grasps of life Be it
the rhythm and most pointed attractions left to spear a kind helm
ship yard war games with no names nor destinies

- Haim Mizrahi

NSTANT

We change, we want...
The instant.
In between we wait.
Time is the visitor
To our instant spoils.

- Joanne de Simone

ℒearn to walk the stroke

It has been a yellow bloom of courage
A splendid host of single prayers
I grieve for left behind expressions
A drive of patterns from a good home
Least is brought presently to grasp
An inhale of property sorting for you and I
Brush stroke to the refuge of stroke rhythm
Even travel chest to chest lone star blast

- Haim Mizrahi

Statues

The pedestal holds the statue
Of a revered someone from the past.
What was his life before
He was carved into bronze
Or stone or copper?
We see the full dress,
The hero, the exalted.
Whom did he love?
Whom did he kill?
Was his posture straight
To be preserved like this?
Did he doubt his worth
To stand forever while
Birds sat on his shoulders
And history shit on his head?

- Joanne de Simone

ℒEAKING POTENCY

Lord of knowledge paper screen full
Place remote of a loving intersection
Leaves abruptly melting feet Partially
Significance reduction Plain field express
Nerve endings slow beak cracking
Blending type set close call prime time
Despite of enable learns runs splits
Nearing a crown removal seems free peeler
Hole of chambers dribble inward expansions
Guise of the recollections pain sleep drive
Timber of an after growth pulses life tracks

- Haim Mizrahi

CHANGES

Laptops, Ipads, drones...
Mother, come back to hear
These words that would
Make you scratch your head!
Dial your friends from a rotary
And wait as it jingles on...
The world is instant oatmeal,
But life goes at its own speed.

- Joanne de Simone

Ahead

Merge of the combined its us
Hearing aid slow pop queen
Oh perfect patronage
An approach most of profound
Meadow plow function
traded early one

- Haim Mizrahi

STARS

When stars fall from the sky
Do they bruise or die in the dark?
Are the sparks of light
Fighting death inevitable
If they ever touch the ground?
It's the same with fame...
A star rises, shines, glitters,
Then it falls, but fame feels pain
In its slow descent.
Stars in the sky are lucky...
We wish upon them,
And yearn for the fate
That calls itself Fame —
Then the star disappears
To avoid the blame.

- Joanne de Simone

$\mathcal{A}$n affair

Tricks of the big seas a trumpet of the grid
Some texture of wondering peak of lush desire
Prime device of goodness bearer
Please perform some hit items in your path
If snobbing becomes a unique aider tip of an iceberg
Proclaiming a getaway trending versions
The pose of presence everybody knows the rules
Honesty and flavor peaking in plain sight
As purchasers of news sellers pointed out

- Haim Mizrahi

*B*EYOND BEAUTY

Mm, mm, beyond beauty...
Look at the butterfly,
Its short life
Lived in living color.
It owns the world
In its brief stay.
Mm, mm, beyond words...
Read some Stein,
It lives forever...
It owns the world.
Both hold beauty
And mystery and wonder.
What is my Mm mm to the world?

- Joanne de Simone

reelance

Pearls shoot the breeze of wind.

Mmm the turn over blinks at night the shift of a royal skin
Posting the scent of mankind level three shrinking in a good Way
polite and eager to apply the knowledge of beast over
The live off screen and portion of freelancing the scan as
Breathtaking pearls shoot the breeze of wind stride no left to Stray
in the gutter of fruit learn brace seasons brought
Partial beam strike heart of gold based blessed
The precious metal deep estimation breath in soulful of the
Country kind the foliage of identity marking of sweet tasty The
pride and all buds of regression brisk of tale livid
Branch extends oh pretty one to the deep soul grasps of life Be it
the rhythm and most pointed attractions left to spear a kind helm
ship yard war games with no names nor destinies

- Haim Mizrahi

𝒲 WORDS

Welcome warmth,
Willows warping,
Without warning,
Whilst woeful
Warbling wrens
Watch when
Wishing wondering
Why with
Workings when
We wake,
Winning wills
Wanting whatever.

- Joanne de Simone

The Fear of Soft Edges

That wasn't there the day before
Self serving in the quest for self regard minus the
Fear of soft
Edges collapsing into the
Void
It needed the
Approval of the watching eyes a self made big
Brother confused and
Incapable of spying on the soft belly of muscles refined
And speaking the language
Of punishment inflicting smooth secrets
It is a characteristic
Of vibrant profiles supportive of speaking for the
Personality vouchers it was easy to
Externalize a swift support of personality not any longer present
To speak a language
Of agreements and expansions minus the sense
Of urgency

- Haim Mizrahi

KING

And then there's the tree
Standing like a king.
He doesn't need a crown,
He attracts birds all around.
And then there are the leaves,
Colors, shapes, breathless,
Do they know they're dying
As they cling to the arms
Of a king and that the wind
Will shake them loose
And leave the king naked?
Yet, with no crown, no color...
Still a king!

- Joanne de Simone

One Two Three

Drowning pig-style forming a fatty sluggish
Harmony with a
Beauty spreading the dingy answer to creativity
Never ending the
Son of a bitch is relentless
Never ending as a manifestation of an ability
Unique as the
Precaution leading to its
Creation and responsible for its well being through the duration
Of lasting in
The whole option lasting and so far it
Seems to be working

- Haim Mizrahi

$\mathcal{W}$EEK

Wednesday's child is filled with woe,
But for this mid-week child
I struggle with the day of the Sun—
The day named for light and starts.
It ends for me at midnight Saturday.
Oh, to be a child of the Sabbath,
That babe that works hard for his living...
It would flip the meaning,
And change the feeling...
I'll take Tuesday and all its Grace.

- Joanne de Simone

Tradition

In the glory of the
Outcome spreads
An ideal scrolling sequence
Tribally gathering
In the new tradition of
Spinning

- Haim Mizrahi

Grime Over Time

From the grime over time
That crushed and cursed,
From the filth of life wanton,
The pollution of swarming flies
Worms on festered flesh...
Of a sudden, with one touch
Renewed, restored, emptied
To give without condition
Sweet breaths of love, light
Of a freedom never known
Cocooned in purple feathers
Of passion purified...

- Joanne de Simone

White pain

A free for all temper of sealed anger
It runs as if the journey turns longer
Where are you color of skin
It's your turn to become kin
Lower under the sliding trip to protest
Pray lastly you remember the slim offset
Today it's our celebration of an esteem
Bravely pointing toward the light beam
So so an awareness preaching selectively
I was the first to last the horror effectively
It's not the pain that turns white
It's not the black that turns pain

- Haim Mizrahi

$\mathcal{I}$ CAN'T TURN

I can't turn
I even burn...
The walls are too close—
They used to be wider,
Or I'm getting bigger.
I also feel water,
It gurgles when I move,
But the space is small
So I can't turn.
What is this tomb
This shifting cocoon?
Oh, wait! It's cracking,
My body is wracking.
I think I'm turning, falling...
It's still so tight.
My eyes sees some light,
Oh, what a fright.
I can't turn...I can't turn back now!

- Joanne de Simone

This bird a lovely bird

This journey
This journey of hers
Mine this bird with this journey
Of hers
My bird is this bird with journeys
Hers
I yield I oblige
I realize bird is bringing
Joy
This one bird of many
Many realizations
Of Wind striking
The feathers of wings sharing

- Haim Mizrahi

$\mathcal{D}$RAGGED

Dragged away from the edition
Of the tradition, ingrained, carved
Into the brain, the train
Of thoughts, process instilled,
Only to find the familiar
Grown stale, and to wail
For the lost or undiscovered—
Given a new promise...
Even if the promise is a lie.
It breaks the tie.

- Joanne de Simone

Smarter

Slow motion in the diversion
Of slim portion temper
Silver lining of
Private bites
Exposure you are a target
Fault hectic minor roll
Arise quorum argue the case now
Every turn lower sum of pity
Sight
To me consumed
Arbitrary yet slash wear and rear
Pulling apart a symbol
Pretty hide in revelations mode trust
Of peep right through
Ground of pickers smarter than a hug of a drive through
In the same token taken inwardly a pose in waiting
To be reconciled as a field cross over
A feel sorry period of a human discharge
And a show of compassion

- Haim Mizrahi

$\mathcal{R}$ANDOM

Sticks, thumbs,
Roses, hope,
Badger, footing,
Fleeting, window,
Clash, neck,
Timing, reach,
Wonder, hollow,
Pallor, crank,
Loud, royal,
Seamless, livid.

- Joanne de Simone

Born

This time it was a ringing sound a spread clone
I thought a while back into the hunger for knowledge
Fighting to find a ratio to that which feels alone
Hop oh hop nearby the company of a personal pledge

Height and all measures at no risk if the thought being spelled
Barking lower that the night of roots so resolve free
Paper cut the thinness far from the pointing paralleled
Way way back blended as a hip portion two three

By by buy bye-bye bright of the nature of seekers eager
Pressed upon the estimate of portion to investment talent
Growth marbles mentioned in conservation pulls a trigger
Emotional it's presiding impression what a temperament

Love to you all bring the message back soon shy purple
Bright eyed posted as its flashy day presenter
May I add to the first born attraction to duality ample
Brave and conscience sorting out softly the imposter

Been blended never liked the look of commitment not yours
(mine)
And maybe almost as a revelation it's service accepted
Dating importance of age relation the great love it pours (prime)
Align wanting close proximate paradoxes slur its holding opted

- Haim Mizrahi

Horse, Pen

This horse, reliable and sturdy,
Black in color, worthy...
Sand, quick sand, climbs.
My horse is a pen...
Its ink black, unworthy.
If it fails, words are lost.
Dig, dig...to no avail.
You're dry, stuck in liquid sand
With an empty writer's hand.

- Joanne de Simone

Shame to limp

Self conscience pebble elevated in pairs soggy proposition
Extended egregiously as
The home front melts parallel to the green light of self
Lovers allowing themselves
To front the self esteem as cover story of the kind the
World resides next to poorly
Performing a bit of the tragedy to come with the notes of a
Gentleman with no shame to limp in the middle of the night
pursuing a shape in the crowd

- Haim Mizrahi

*Y*ou TOO I WE

In the voice of Haim, as I hear it...

Papa is the dreamcatcher the sentry
The keeper of your sheltered slumber
Throughout the night where only
Butterfly kisses brush by leaving
Sweet songs from the Sandman
Sleep deep on waves that secure
And set free your young mind to dream
While in the dark Papa holds your hand

- Joanne de Simone

You too I we

In the voice of Joanne as I hear it...

When we got together you seemed sad
Already thinking of the days to come
A blend of thoughts and cozy wraps
Flew lower than I have anticipated
You were too a figure of observation
I know we will carry on with the burden
And challenges will spring happily
Surrounding an image of grammar
Only to fly steady and willingly entering
A sight of promise and hopping
You were I so we too flourished
I believe so

- Haim Mizrahi

Unleash the letters from your soul...

- J. de

About The Author

HAIM MIZRAHI

The work of Israeli Haim Mizrahi leaps into existence and stirs his reader, viewer or listener with an impeccable energy.

No matter what the medium, be it painting, writing or freestyle jazz, Mr. Mizrahi draws together the tones and rhythms and thoughts of his life as the artist, the soldier, and the working man.

Since 1999, Haim has been the host of *Hello, Hello* at LTV-East Hampton's Public Access Television, telecast throughout Long Island and Connecticut, and has been a producer at the network since 1987.

His audiences here and in Jerusalem are treated, continually, to the feast of his passion and the instinct for the incredible.

From a poet that writes from a streaming sensibility, he declares, "Poetry is the crown of the passage."

Haim is an artistic original whose work runs the gamut of styles simply because of his detachment from the rules that do not apply to a free mind and spirit.

Haim Mizrahi's exhibits can be viewed in galleries from East Hampton to NYC to Tel-Aviv.

He is a resident of East Hampton,

Check his FACEBOOK and INSTAGRAM pages for the upcoming events.

JOANNE DE SIMONE

*J*oanne is an author, poet, film historian, and award winning playwright.

She is the author of two Young Adult books, *The Metro Cats: Life in the Core of the Big Apple*, and *The Peculiar Plight of Milicent Wryght*, urban tales set in Manhattan. Other books include *Spills from a Quill* (poetry and prose), *Lovers. Husbands. Strangers.* (a Baby Boomer's chronicle of lust, love and one night stands), and soon to be released *Songs from Under the El: Memories of Life in the Dark.*

Her most recent works include a whimsical pocket-sized *Mating Habits Couples Guide A-Z*, and co-authorship of *Inside Out Yoga* with Sandra K., actress/talk show host of *Café with Sandra K.* at LTV, EH.

Joanne's twelve plays will be assembled in a collection to be published in late 2021. Her film review column appeared in the Fire Island News from 1998-2003. de Simone's work has been published in various magazines, publications and film journals.

Joanne is a proud Board member of the Veronica Moscoso Foundation, with grass roots educational facilities in the U.S. and South America, where she has donated her YA books. Joanne will teach a creative writing course for teens in Fall 2021. She is currently the host of *Notes & Notions from The Writing Desk* on LTV, East Hampton's Public Access Television.

She is also a member of the Dramatists Guild, the English Speaking Union, Shakespeare Guild, Episcopal Actors Guild, Drama League, TRU, and FIJET (world federation of journalist and writers); judge at Hudson River Classics Stage Play Competition

Joanne holds a B.A. in Literature, Film and Creative Writing.

She recently launched STRAMAL (St. Rita and Archangel Metatron Arts League) a 501c3 non-profit organization, created to inspire and encourage 'tweens' and teens to pursue their creative endeavors. Visit www.stramal.com.

Follow Joanne on FACEBOOK and INSTAGRAM

A special thanks to Haim Mizrahi for his magnetic energy that inspired these poems, all written live, on the air, during his LTV-EH show, *Hello Hello*.

Big thanks to Michael D. Clark and all the wonderful staff at LTV for their support and encouragement.

Printed in the United States
by Baker & Taylor Publisher Services